ABOUT THIS BOOK

Black-tailed prairie dogs make
their homes in the flat country of
the Great Plains. These plump
little animals live in extended
families and spend much time
kissing and grooming each
other. They work together to
build comfortable underground
burrows and to protect
themselves from their enemies.
Coyotes, ferrets, eagles, and
badgers all live close by. Open
this book and you will find that
a lot goes on in a prairie dog town.

a LET ME READ book

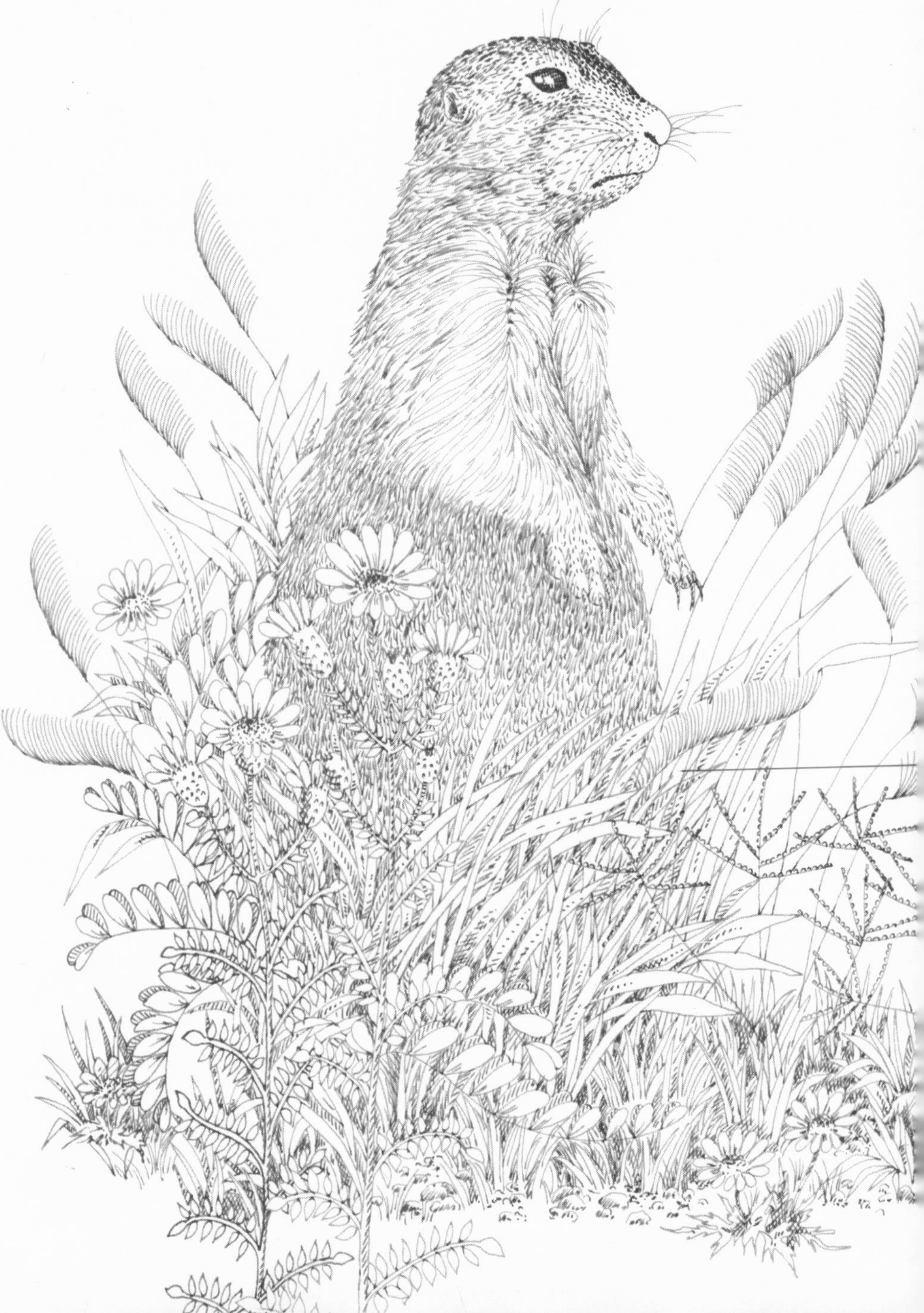

Come Visit a Prairie Dog Town

by Eugenia Alston

Illustrated by St. Tamara

Harcourt Brace Jovanovich
New York and London

Printed in the United States of America

First edition

B C D E F G H I J K

Library of Congress Cataloging in Publication Data

Alston, Eugenia.
    Come visit a prairie dog town.

    (A Let me read book)
    SUMMARY: Describes a prairie dog coterie, or family, focusing on the characteristics and behavior of its members at different ages and seasons.
    1. Prairie-dogs—Juvenile literature.
[1. Prairie dogs]   I. St. Tamara.   II. Title.
QL737.R68A38   599'.3232   75-37005
ISBN 0-15-219480-0
ISBN 0-15-219481-9 pbk.

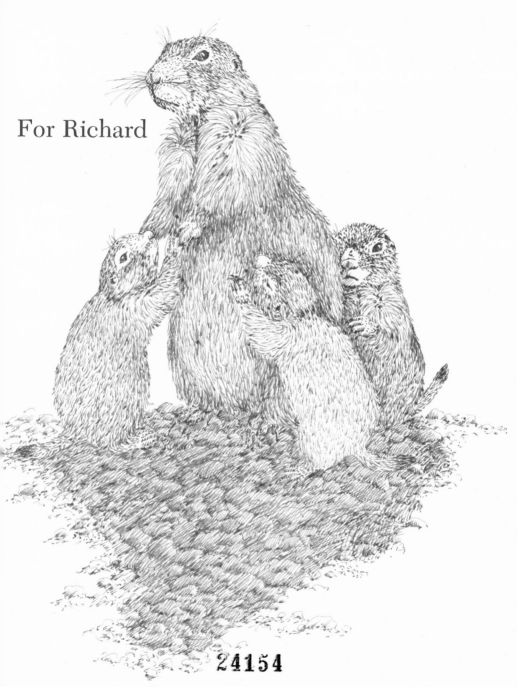

For Richard

Summer days are learning days in a prairie dog town. By living the way they always do, the older prairie dogs show the young how to survive.

If you want to watch prairie dogs, you'll have to be very quiet. When you first visit their town, you might hear a bark. Then you might see little dark tails disappear into the ground. The prairie dogs saw you coming.

But stay awhile, because prairie dogs
are curious. They will come out of
their underground burrows to see
what is going on. And a lot goes on in
a prairie dog town.

Black-tailed prairie dogs live in the
flat country of the Great Plains. Their
towns look like craters on the moon.
All you can see are low dirt mounds,
with grass growing between them.

In this town, only one prairie dog is awake. His little tan head is showing above a mound. It is early morning, and the sky is still dark overhead. In the east, where the sun will rise, it is as pink as the inside of a seashell.

"Chirk!" The little prairie dog gives a bark. He has seen a dark moving shape coming out of a mound. The prairie dog disappears into his hole.

The dark shape moves between the mounds like a rippling shadow. It is a black-footed ferret, and she carries a young prairie dog in her teeth.

This rare little animal has a mask of dark fur around her bright eyes, and her coat is the color of coffee with cream. She lives in an old prairie dog burrow at the edge of the town.

The mother ferret has been hunting all night. At last she has caught a prairie dog, and she is taking it home to her three hungry young. She will feed them and stay with them during the day, while the prairie dogs are awake.

The sun is higher now, and more prairie dogs have appeared. Some are nibbling at the grasses, and some sit upright on the mounds. These plump little ground squirrels are only about twelve inches high, but from the mounds they can see a long way. They are little sentinels at their lookout posts.

There is a female prairie dog coming
out of her burrow. She goes to a male
on a mound nearby. These prairie
dogs greet with a "kiss." They bare
their teeth, and the female touches
her mouth to his. Prairie dogs use the
kiss to recognize each other.

This female is a mother, and she belongs to the male's coterie. A coterie is a prairie dog family. This coterie has one father, three mothers, and sixteen young prairie dogs. Twelve were born three months ago, in April, and the other four are one year old.

The land where the coterie lives is called a territory. Aboveground, you may see nothing but mounds, but these mounds lead to burrows underground. A burrow is a system of tunnels. At one end of the tunnel there may be a hole without a mound. That is the prairie dogs' back door.

Members of the coterie keep other prairie dogs out of their territory. Each territory has enough food to feed the coterie. Prairie dogs eat grasses and thistles and seeds, and sometimes a grasshopper. They get water from the plants they eat.

In the burrows, the adult prairie dogs
have small chambers for sleeping.
Last spring, each mother carried grass
into her chamber and lined it to make
a nest. She gave birth to her young
there, and then she let no one come
near, not even the father.

But now the little prairie dogs are growing up. They run from one burrow to another, and sometimes they sleep in different nests. They even nurse different mothers. No one minds. Members of a coterie are one big happy family.

The female takes the male's place on the mound. Her little paws are folded on her chest. She stands on lookout while the male makes his territorial rounds.

There is no boundary to the territory that a person can see. Every young prairie dog learns its territory from older prairie dogs. If you want to find the boundary, watch the male as he goes on his rounds.

The male sees another prairie dog. The two plump animals crawl toward each other. They bare their teeth to greet with a kiss. Suddenly, the other prairie dog turns and races home. He is off his territory. He belongs to the coterie next door. The owner chases the intruder a little and bites him on the rump, but prairie dogs don't really hurt each other.

Here comes a young prairie dog. When the male does not greet it with a kiss, the youngster runs away. Earlier in the summer, the male would have treated the young one like one of his own. In their first few months, the little prairie dogs often visit the coteries next door. But now it is July. It is time for the youngsters to learn about territories.

Here are more small prairie dogs. The
male is their father. He greets them
all with kisses. The youngsters wiggle
and kiss and beg to be groomed. The
father grooms their fur by stroking it
with his paws. Some lie on their backs
while he grooms their bellies. The
young ones kiss each other, and they
groom each other, too. They are
having a wonderful time.

But their father has other things to do.
Gently, he pushes the young ones
away. Some run off. If they run too far,
they will enter another coterie, and
they will be chased home.

The male moves on. He sees another
male, and he chases this intruder too.
Then he stands on his hind feet and
gives a call.

"Wheeooo! Wheeooo! Wheeeoooooo!"
The call says, "This is my territory!"
Around the town, other prairie dogs
echo the sound.

"Wheeooo! Wheeoooooo!" Each one is
saying the same thing. The young
ones say it so hard that sometimes
they topple over. "Wheeooo!"
Kerplop.

The male passes one burrow without stopping. It is an old prairie dog hole. Burrowing owls live there now. They, too, are raising their young. Sometimes the owls try to catch a small prairie dog. In the spring, a female prairie dog stole an owl egg and ate it. But most of the time, the owls hunt away from their home, and the two families leave each other alone.

Suddenly, the male hears a warning
bark. Many prairie dogs join in the
call. The male sits up, and he sees
three bison moving toward the town.
The prairie dogs are running for their
burrows, getting out of the bisons'
way.

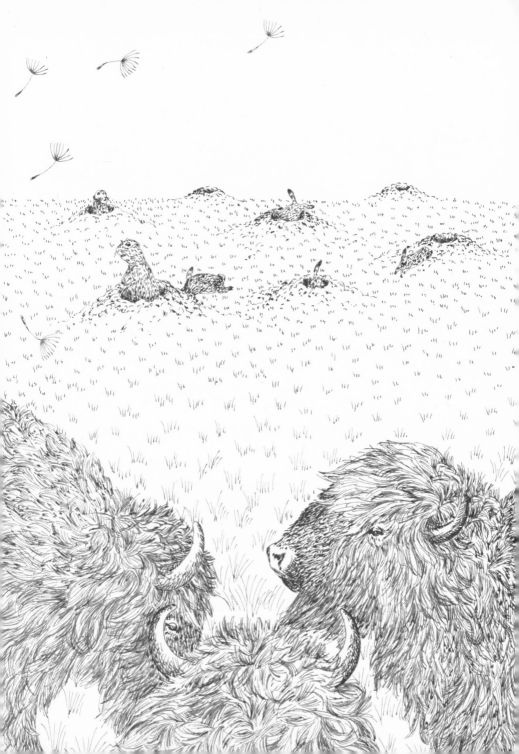

The male scampers into his hole. Bison love prairie dog towns. They roll in the dirt to keep cool and to keep insects away. One old bison stamps at a hole. He paws the mound and spreads dirt around. His heavy body drops slowly to the ground. Dust rises around him in a cloud. The bison rolls onto his back and rubs more dust in his shoulders. He sits up in the cloud of dust he has made. He is feeling very good.

The male prairie dog and his family
wait underground. When everything
is quiet, they follow the tunnels and
go outside. The prairie dog burrow is
a mess. The mound is mashed flat,
and the tunnel is full of dirt. The old
bison is grazing nearby. He doesn't
seem the least bit sorry.

The prairie dog family goes to work. The little animals push loose dirt out of the tunnel. They scrape the soil back into a mound. They pack it down with their heads. When they pass each other, they sometimes stop to kiss. Everyone cooperates. Soon the mound is together again.

Mounds are important for prairie
dogs. Standing on their mounds, the
prairie dogs are always watching.
They watch for eagles that may dip
out of the sky.

They watch for coyotes that may
pounce on them.

They watch for badgers that will dig
into their tunnels.

And they watch for the black-footed ferret.

Prairie dog mounds also catch rain. The rain drains off the mound, away from the tunnel. The tunnel also has a trap to keep out the rain. The tunnel goes down, and then it turns up again. Prairie dogs in their burrows stay warm and dry. In winter, they can keep warm in their underground homes and come out only on sunny days.

Around the town, the prairie dogs are nibbling at grasses and digging new tunnels. They spend most of their time eating and digging and grooming. Grooming helps prairie dogs recognize each other, just as kissing does. Only members of the same coterie groom each other. But the little ones like grooming so much that they get to be pests.

As the young ones grow up, food on the territory gets scarce. During the summer, some of the ones born last year move away. They claim new territories and dig new burrows at the edge of the town. Next spring, these prairie dogs will be raising families of their own.

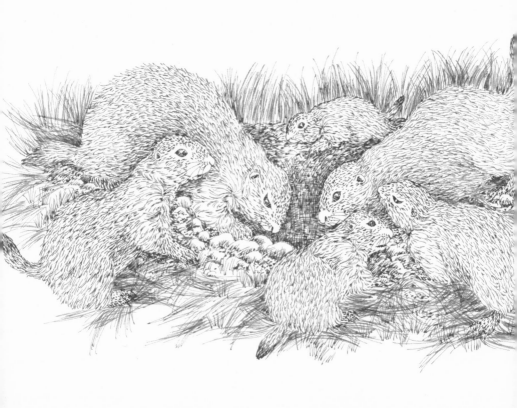

Sometimes the parents leave the old
territory and the ones born last year
stay. Then the young ones learn about
living on a territory from the big
brothers and sisters that stay behind.
Knowing the territory is the prairie
dog's way of life.

When prairie dogs dig tunnels, they
bring air into the soil. The air is good
for insects and plants that live and
grow there. Prairie dogs also leave
their droppings underground.
Droppings make the soil fertile, so
many plants can grow.

Around their burrows, the prairie dogs cut down the tall grasses so they can watch for enemies. The weeds and grasses that grow back have plenty of seeds. They are good food for the prairie dogs and other small animals. Other animals also use the prairie dog tunnels. Mice and rabbits sometimes hide there, and little snakes stay cool there during the hot part of the day. The prairie dog doesn't mind. As long as it is safe from enemies, it leaves other animals alone.

Evening is coming to the flat prairie land. All the prairie dogs gather aboveground. The young ones run and play, and the older ones groom each other or nibble on grasses. All across the town, prairie dogs watch from their mounds.

A coyote calls on a distant hill. The sun is dropping in the sky. Soon the prairie dogs will crawl into their burrows and sleep.

Soon also, the mother ferret will come
out of her hole. When it is dark, she
will lead her young on a hunt. In
autumn, little ferrets leave their
mothers, and they must be able to find
their own food by then.

By watching their mother, the little ferrets learn to hunt. In the prairie dog family, the young ones learn to live in a different way. Each kind of animal has a pattern for survival. Each prepares its offspring for growing up in the best way it can.

Eugenia Alston grew up in Alabama and graduated from the University of North Carolina with honors in writing. She has been an editor for several New York publishers and, after working on a nature series for two years, became fascinated with animal behavior. Ms. Alston is the author of *Rainy-Day Chimpanzees.*

St. Tamara was born in Byelorussia and emigrated to the United States in 1950. She has a Master of Fine Arts from Columbia University and has had her artwork widely exhibited. St. Tamara has illustrated books for both adults and children.